FOOD

FRUIT

Jillian Powell

WAYLAND

Titles in the series

BREAD   EGGS   FISH   FRUIT
MILK   PASTA   POTATOES
POULTRY   RICE   VEGETABLES

First published in 1996 by Wayland (Publishers) Ltd
61 Western Road, Hove, East Sussex, BN3 1JD, England

© 1996 Wayland (Publishers) Ltd

Series Editor: Sarah Doughty
Editor: Liz Harman
Design: Jean Wheeler
Illustration: Peter Bull
Cover: Zul Mukhida – assistant photostylist Bridget Tily

British Library Cataloguing in Publication Data
Powell, Jillian
Fruit. – (Food)
1. Fruit – Juvenile literature
2. Cookery (Fruit) – Juvenile literature
I. Title
641.3'4

ISBN 0 7502 1974 2

Typeset by Jean Wheeler

Printed and bound in Italy by L.E.G.O. S.p.A., Vicenza

Picture acknowledgements

Cephas 4, 6 (top), 9 (top), 11 (left), 12, 14 (both), 15 (top), 16 (bottom), 17 (both), 18 (bottom), 19 (both), 20 (both), 21 (both), 22 (both), 23 (both), 24; Chapel Studios 5 (top), 8–9 (bottom), 10 (right), 25 (bottom); Cranberry Information Bureau/Ocean Spray Cranberries Ltd. 7 (bottom) and 15 (bottom); James Davis Travel Photography 10 (left); Dried Fruit Information Service 13 (bottom), 16 (top); Mary Evans 7 (top), 8 (left), 25 (top); Eye Ubiquitous 5 (bottom), 11 (right); Michael Holford 6 (bottom); Wayland Picture Library title page, contents page, 13 (top and middle), 18 (top).

Contents

Fantastic fruit   4
The first fruits   6
Fruit in the past   8
What is fruit?   10
The food in fruit   12
How fruit grows   14
Preserving fruit   16
Fruit products   18
Cooking with fruit   20
Fruit dishes from around the world   22
Fruit legends and customs   24
Fruit recipes for you to try   26
Glossary   30
Books to read   31
Index   32

Fantastic fruit

Fruit is one of our oldest and most varied natural foods. Fruits come in every size, shape and colour, from tiny blackcurrants to watermelons bigger than footballs.

A fruit is the fleshy part of a plant which protects the seeds. Some foods that we think of as vegetables are really fruits. They include tomatoes, aubergines, olives, avocado pears and cucumbers. Rhubarb, which we use as a fruit, is really a vegetable because it is the stem of the plant that we eat.

Different types of fruit have different tastes and appearances. Some fruits, like apples, are hard and crunchy. Others, like peaches and mangoes, are soft and juicy. Some have smooth skins that we can eat, like grapes, cherries and plums. Others have to be peeled, like oranges, lemons, bananas and pineapples.

Fruits grow on trees and bushes. Fruit is an important food for people and for wild animals and birds.

Fruit can be eaten in lots of different ways. It can be served raw or cooked and in sweet or savoury dishes. Fruit can be used in soups, stews and salads, jellies, pies and cakes, or made into juice, squash and tea.

▲ Nuts are a dry kind of fruit with a hard shell. These are almonds growing on a tree in Sri Lanka.

Although lots of fruits are good to eat, some types of berries and fruits can be poisonous. They could make you ill or even kill you. Never eat a fruit unless you know that it is safe to eat. Some people can become ill if they eat some kinds of nut. We call this an allergy.

◀ Fruits like watermelon contain up to 90 per cent water, which makes them refreshing to eat, especially in hot weather.

The first fruits

People have been eating fruit for thousands of years. The earliest peoples gathered the fruit and nuts of wild plants. By about 4,000 BC, fruits including dates, figs, grapes, olives and pomegranates were being grown and harvested.

The ancient Greeks and Romans used fruit to sweeten fish and meat dishes. Fruit was not usually eaten raw because doctors believed it caused disease. The Romans learned how to dry and preserve fruits. They turned grapes into raisins and wine, and stored other fruits in clay pots, with honey, salt water or vinegar.

▲ The date palm is one of the most ancient trees in the world.

▶ The ancient Egyptians grew grapes and learned to ferment them to make wine. This painting in a tomb shows a husband and wife standing under their grape vines.

In the Middle Ages, cooks used dry fruits like prunes, raisins and currants in meat and fish stews and pies as well as cakes and puddings. Doctors still believed raw fruit was dangerous. When a very dangerous disease called the plague was spreading in London, the sale of fresh fruits in the street was banned.

In the sixteenth century, fruit was preserved in sugar and used in jams, jellies and a dish called flummery, which was made with spiced cream and set in a mould.

In the sixteenth century, there was a fashion for coloured fruit dishes. Quinces and pears were cooked with red wine and green apple pies were made by stewing the apples in copper pans with vine leaves. Acid from the fruit reacted with the metal of the pan to turn the fruit green.

▲ People picking grapes at a French vineyard in the fifteenth century.

Cranberries first grew wild in North America. The Amerindians used them for food and medicine and to dye clothes and feathers. The Amerindians showed the Pilgrim Fathers where to gather cranberries and they feasted on them at the first Thanksgiving in 1621. Cranberries are still a traditional part of the Thanksgiving meal in the USA.

Fruit in the past

In the eighteenth century, doctors realised that raw fruit was a healthy food. By the end of the century, the British Navy was giving lemon and lime juice to sailors on long sea voyages, to stop them getting scurvy, a disease caused by lack of Vitamin C.

◀ In the eighteenth century, orange sellers like this woman sold oranges as snacks in the street and at theatres.

In cooking, desserts called fools were made with fresh fruit, milk and cream. Quinces, pears and plums were made into marmalade, which was often so thick that it had to be cut with a knife. Fashionable fruit puddings included melon dyed green with spinach juice and peaches poached in red wine or cochineal (a red dye from a kind of beetle).

◀ These stone pineapples are a symbol of wealth. They are on the gates of a vineyard in France, which are also carved with grapes.

Pineapples were first brought to Europe from South America in the sixteenth century. They became very popular in England and rich people grew pineapples in hot houses.
A pineapple on a coat of arms or a gate post was a symbol of wealth. In the 1870s, pineapples began to arrive fresh from the West Indies on steam ships.

Rich fruit cakes began to be made for celebrations like birthdays, weddings and Christmas. With the arrival of more tropical fruits on steam ships in the nineteenth century, and the invention of canning by about 1900, the range of available fruits increased.

◀ Pears being poached in red wine to turn them red. This dish was popular in the eighteenth century.

What is fruit?

A fruit is the part of a plant that protects the seeds. Fruits grow when the flowers have been fertilized. Male pollen grains reach the ovule (the female part of a flower) and fertilize it, producing a seed. A fruit then grows to protect and feed the seed. Nuts protect their seed or kernel inside a hard shell.

▲ Wild birds and animals, like this grey squirrel, eat fruit, nuts and seeds. They spread the seeds around by passing them through their bodies.

Some fruits can grow in most countries of the world. Others need a certain climate to grow well. Tropical fruits like bananas, pineapples and mangoes need lots of rain and hot sunshine to grow. Fruits like apples, pears and raspberries grow in much cooler, temperate climates. Dates grow in hot, dry desert lands.

◀ Bananas are grown on plantations in tropical countries. Each tree can bear up to 200 bananas in clusters called 'hands'.

Fruits can be grouped into families, like the citrus family, which contains oranges, lemons, limes and grapefruit. We can also group together hard and crunchy fruits or soft and juicy fruits.

Fruits like plums, peaches and avocado pears have one big seed or stone inside. Others, like apples, melons and grapes, have lots of pips or seeds. Berries are fruits which contain small seeds inside their soft flesh. They include tomatoes, gooseberries, raspberries and blackcurrants. Their seeds are so tiny that we can eat them.

◀ Apricots come from the group of fruits that contain one hard stone. Inside the stone is a soft kernel.

▶ Some fruits, like these pomegranates, kiwi fruits and passionfruits have small edible seeds.

The food in fruit

Fruit provides a healthy snack or part of a meal and is refreshing, healthy and good to eat.

Fresh fruits contain substances called anti-oxidants (including Vitamins C and E), which help keep our body cells healthy and prevent disease.

Different fruits contain different nutrients but most contain lots of the vitamins and minerals we need to keep us healthy.

Bananas are a good source of energy because they are rich in carbohydrate. They also contain Vitamins A, B and C.

Fruits like apples, pears, pawpaws and strawberries contain fibre, which helps us to digest food and pass it through our bodies.

▲ Crunchy fruits like apples help to keep our teeth and gums healthy.

Tennis players often eat bananas during long matches. This is because bananas contain lots of potassium, which helps to stop cramp.

Apples contain a chemical called pectin, which helps to protect against heart disease caused by too much cholesterol in our bodies. The pectin gets into the bloodstream, and sticks to the cholesterol, helping the blood to flow around the body.

◀ Freshly squeezed fruit juice is a good source of Vitamin C.

▼ Fruits containing lots of Vitamin C include citrus fruits like these, as well as kiwi fruits, redcurrants and blackcurrants. Vitamin C helps us fight colds and other illnesses.

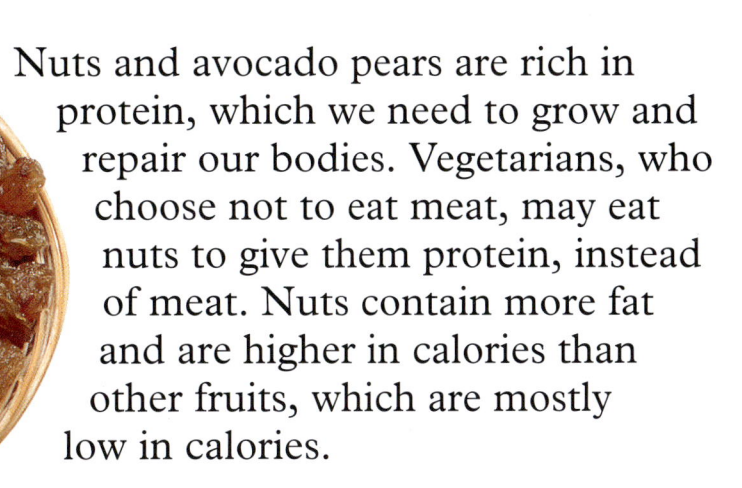

Nuts and avocado pears are rich in protein, which we need to grow and repair our bodies. Vegetarians, who choose not to eat meat, may eat nuts to give them protein, instead of meat. Nuts contain more fat and are higher in calories than other fruits, which are mostly low in calories.

◀ Fruits that are high in sugar include dates and dried fruits like these sultanas. They are a good source of energy.

How fruit grows

Fruit is grown all over the world, in gardens, orchards, fruit farms and plantations. It also grows wild in forests, woods and hedgerows.

Fruit trees and bushes are planted and pruned in the winter, when they have no leaves. Farmers use animal manure or chemicals to feed fruit plants, which helps them to produce a good crop.

In spring, when fruit trees and bushes come into flower, farmers must make sure the flowers are fertilized. Some farmers keep bees to carry pollen from flower to flower.

Once fruits have formed, the farmer may spray the plants with chemicals, which fight pests and diseases. Organic farmers prefer not to use chemicals as they believe they can harm people and the environment.

▲ A man pruning apple trees in Japan. Pruning allows light and air to reach new shoots, which start to grow in spring.

▶ Peach trees in an Italian orchard being sprayed to prevent pests and diseases.

Sunshine helps fruits to grow and ripen. Some fruits, such as strawberries, ripen in summer. Others, like apples and pears, ripen in autumn. It is important to pick fruit at the right time. Fruits like pineapples are picked when they are ripe and sweet. Other fruits, like bananas, are picked when they are unripe, because they continue to ripen after picking. Grapes have to be picked when they contain the right amount of sugar for wine making.

▲ It is very important that fruit trees and bushes have enough water. In dry weather, farmers may need to water their crops.

All fruit must be picked carefully so that it is not damaged. Some fruits can be harvested by special machines which shake the bushes and gather up the fruits. Many fruits are picked by hand.

Fruit must be stored in cool, dry sheds. Some farmers spray it with chemicals to stop it rotting. Fruit may be washed and dried by warm air before being sorted by size, weight and quality. Packers check the fruit before packing it in boxes to be sold or taken to factories for processing. Fruit must be transported quickly so that it stays fresh.

A cranberry contains four pockets of air. This means that it can float. Sometimes, farmers harvest cranberries by flooding the fields. The cranberries are knocked off the plants and a machine skims the floating cranberries off the top of the water.

Preserving fruit

There are many ways of preserving fruit once it has been picked. If it is not preserved, bacteria will feed on sugar in the fruit and it will rot.

Bacteria need water to live so one way of preserving fruit is to dry it. Fruit such as dates, figs, apples and pears can be dried in the sunshine or in hot-air tunnels. This removes up to 75 per cent of the water from the fruit. Dried fruit is more chewy than fresh fruit, and is very nutritious. Dried fruit may be ready to eat or may need soaking in water before use.

Lemon juice can be used to stop sliced fruits turning brown when they react with in the air. The acidity in the citrus juice also improves flavour.

◀ Raisins, sultanas and currants are different types of dried grapes.

▼ In the hot sun of Victoria, Australia, these grapes are being dried to make sultanas.

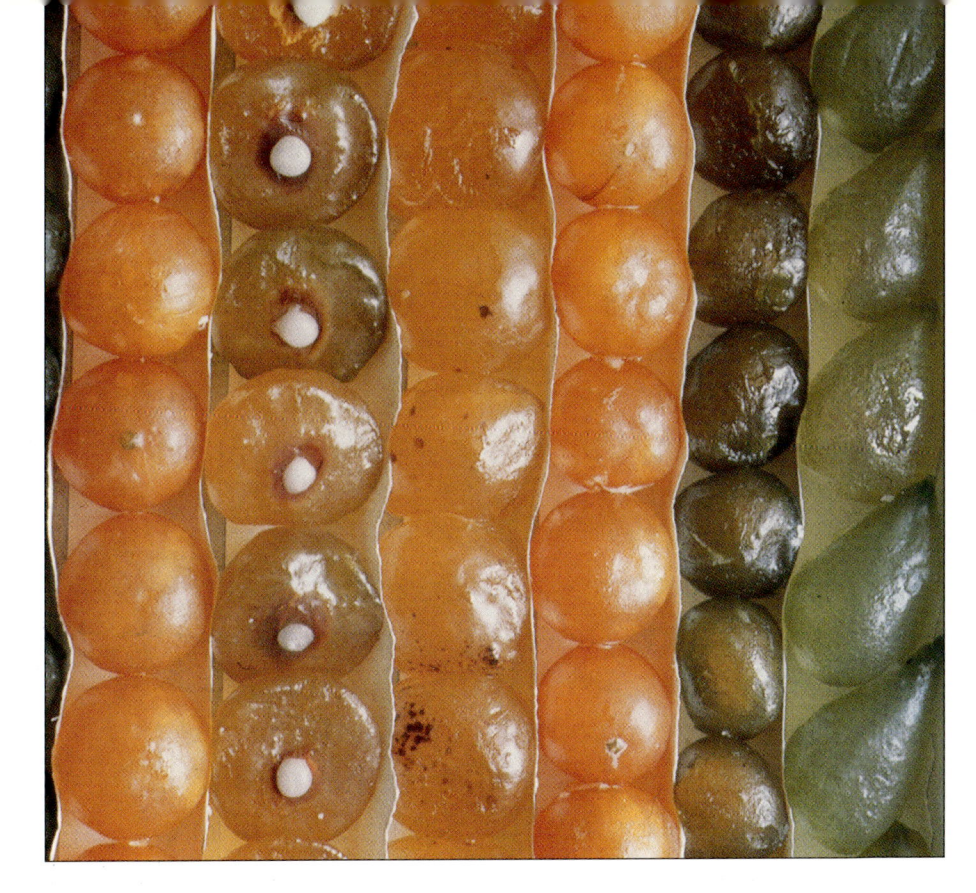

◀ Fruit can be preserved by sugar. Candied or crystallized fruit like this has had most of its water replaced by sugar. Making jam, curd or marmalade is another way of preserving fruit using sugar.

Fruit may be canned in sugar syrup or fruit juice. The fruit is part-cooked then sealed in airtight metal cans, which are heated to kill bacteria.

Some fruits can be frozen. Raspberries and cherries freeze well, but other fruits like strawberries can lose their shape and texture.

Fruit can be bottled in vinegar, wine or spirits or made into spicy chutneys and pickles. Rumtopf is a German pot of fruits preserved in rum. In the West Indies, tropical fruits are bottled with rum and spices and pickled limes are sold as snacks in the street.

▼ Tomatoes being prepared for canning at a factory in Italy.

Fruit products

Fruit is processed into many different products at food processing factories. The fruit is cooked or dried and used to make pies, tarts, biscuits, cakes, puddings, mousses, fools, yoghurt and ice-cream.

Fruit may also be crushed and used to make jellies, sauces, ketchups, jams and marmalades. Fruit pulp, which is left over when fruits have been crushed, is used in animal feed. Lemon oil may be used in cosmetics or household cleaners such as cream cleaners and washing-up liquid.

Some fruits, like raspberries, can be used to make vinegar and fruit teas. Fruit juice is packed in bottles or cartons and used to make squashes and other fruit drinks.

▲ Dried fruits are often added to breakfast cereals like this muesli. Some people also like to add slices of fresh fruit to their cereals.

▶ A selection of colourful fruit juice drinks.

◀ A machine crushing apples for cider-making in Somerset, England.

To make cider, yeast is added to apple juice which is then left to ferment in cider vats for several weeks. Some cider is distilled, to make apple brandy, called calvados in France, and applejack in the USA. Wine is made by crushing grapes and adding yeast which ferments the sugar in the fruit, turning it to alcohol.

Nuts are roasted and crushed for use in ice-cream, yogurt, nougat, patés, burgers and sausages. The oil from nuts is used for cooking, and to make margarine, soap, hand cream, paint and varnish. Almonds and coconut are crushed to make a kind of milk.

▼ Fruit jams, made by cooking summer fruits with sugar.

Coconut flesh and milk can be used for cooking fish and meat, and in sweets, cakes and biscuits. Coconut oil is used in cosmetics such as soap and hand cream, and the thick fibre, called coir, can be used to make mats, rope and garden compost.

Cooking with fruit

There are many simple ways of cooking fruit. Fruits like apples and bananas can be baked in the oven or fried in a little butter.

Pears, apples and softer fruits like apricots and peaches can be poached in juice, syrup or wine. Many fruits can be stewed with sugar or honey until they are soft.

Nuts can be roasted in an oven or toasted under the grill. Cashew nuts must be roasted before they are safe to eat.

▲ Apples can be cored and filled with dried fruit, butter, sugar and spices and baked in the oven for a delicious dessert.

▼ Banana fritters made from bananas fried with butter and sugar.

Fruit is made into many kinds of sweet dishes all over the world, such as American blueberry muffins and apple pie, German Black Forest gateau, Austrian strudel and Danish pastries. Fruits are also used to make ice-cream, yoghurt, mousses, jelly, fruit salad, sauces, biscuits and sweets.

In Eastern, Indian, African and Caribbean cooking, fruit is used in many savoury dishes. Unripe fruits including pawpaws, mangoes, bananas and plantains are used in soups, stews and curries. In the East, fish and meat is often cooked in coconut milk.

In the Middle East, apricots and prunes are cooked with lamb, and soups and stews are flavoured with pomegranate juice or whole lemons and limes. Fruits like quinces may be stuffed with spicy meat fillings.

In Western cooking, fruit for savoury dishes is mainly used in sauces, such as cranberry with turkey, apple with pork and cherry with duck. Gammon may be served with pineapple and lemon is used to flavour and garnish fish.

◀ Sweet and savoury flavours go together well in this dish made with duck and apricots.

Pineapple, pawpaw and kiwi fruit can all help to make meat more tender because they contain chemicals which can break down protein. These fruits cannot be used fresh in jelly because these chemicals prevent the jelly from setting.

◀ West Indian dishes flavoured with bananas and limes.

Fruit dishes from around the world

In eastern Europe, Germany and Scandinavia, fruit is made into soups, such as Hungarian cherry soup and German 'heaven and earth' soup made from apples and potatoes.

In Africa, soup is made from bananas or pawpaws. Bananas, plantains and coconuts are used in chicken and beef stews. Plantain chips are more popular than potato chips.

▲ Clafoutis, a French dish made by baking black cherries in a rich pancake batter.

The Caribbean dish of Creole bananas is made from bananas cooked with salt fish, pork, onions, tomatoes, peppers and coconut milk. Popular desserts include lime pie, pawpaw custard, and guavas cooked in sugar syrup, served with salty cheese.

▶ The Mexican dish of guacamole is made by crushing avocado pears with tomatoes, chilli peppers, lemon juice and garlic.

In the West Indies, pickled limes are chopped into salads and eaten with fried shark. Pepper mangoes are a popular street snack made by bottling mangoes with chilli peppers in salted water.

In Asia, meals often end with fresh fruit. In Korea, slices of fruit are eaten with small forks from a dish in the middle of the table. In Thailand, chefs carve fruits like pawpaws and mangoes into beautiful flower shapes.

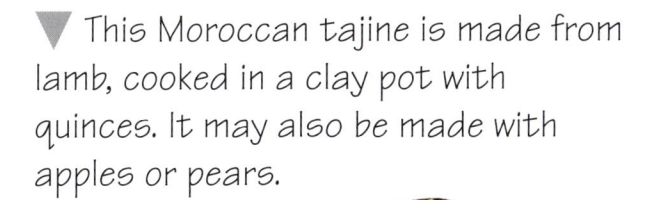

▼ This Moroccan tajine is made from lamb, cooked in a clay pot with quinces. It may also be made with apples or pears.

▲ A feast of Caribbean dishes, including pineapple and lime salad, lime tart with coconut and lime jelly.

Faisinjan is a Middle Eastern dish of duck or lamb cooked with walnuts and pomegranate juice. Mishmishaya is a traditional recipe for lamb stewed with apricots.

American Waldorf salad is made from apples, walnuts, celery, raisins and lettuce.

The Russian Easter cake Pashka is made with dried fruits, sour cream and cream cheese. The cake is baked in a tall mould and decorated with candied fruits.

Fruit legends and customs

Fruit plays a part in stories, legends, folklore, festivals and religion. In the Christian Bible, Eve tempted Adam with an apple. Apples appear in classical legends, and fairytales like Snow White. In Norse and Arabian mythology, magic apples have the power to give life forever and even bring people back to life.

In China, peaches are a symbol of living forever and a token of friendship. Mangoes are important in Hindu and Buddhist belief. Buddha meditated in a mango grove.

Pomegranates are an ancient symbol of fertility and wealth in many cultures because of their many seeds. In medieval times, they were pictured on coats of arms and on kings' and priests' robes.

Apple bobbing is traditional for Hallowe'en, recalling a Roman festival held at the beginning of November to celebrate Pomona, goddess of fruits and seeds. In the USA, pumpkin pie is a traditional dish at the Thanksgiving feast.

▲ These people are dressed up for the Chinese Moon Festival in September, which celebrates an ancient legend. At the festival, moon-shaped fruits like peaches and melons are eaten.

Fruit features in many New Year customs. In the English New Year tradition of wassailing, people dance and sing round fruit trees, lighting torches and sprinkling the trees with cider or crumbs of food. This is to feed the trees and help them make more fruit.

◀ Wassailing apple trees with hot cider in England during the nineteenth century.

▼ Dried limes hanging on a balcony in India to bring good luck.

At New Year in India, lemons and limes are left in baskets on doorsteps to bring luck to friends and neighbours. The Chinese eat cherries, apples and tomatoes because red is their lucky colour. In Greece and Spain, it is traditional to eat a grape on each stroke as the clock chimes midnight, to bring 12 months of good luck. Jewish people dip sliced apples in honey, to bring a sweet New Year.

Fruit recipes for you to try

Apple and bacon burgers

To serve two to four people you will need:

30 g butter
a small onion, chopped
3 or 4 cold cooked potatoes, mashed
2 apples, peeled, cored and chopped
4 rashers of bacon, chopped
a pinch of salt and pepper
1 small egg, beaten
4 tablespoons cooking oil

1 Ask an adult to help you to melt the butter gently in a frying pan. Fry the onion for about 5–10 minutes until it is soft.

2 Put the onion in a bowl with the mashed potato and mix together well.

3 Stir in the chopped apples and bacon, and add a pinch of salt and pepper.

4 Now add just enough of the beaten egg until the mixture sticks together well.

5 Carefully divide up the mixture into balls, then flatten each ball into a patty shape.

6 Ask an adult to help you to heat the oil gently in the frying pan. Fry the patties gently on both sides until they are golden.

Serve with fresh vegetables or a salad.

Banana and pineapple crumble

To serve four people you will need:

4 bananas, peeled and cut into chunks
4 slices of fresh or tinned pineapple, cut into chunks
the grated rind of an orange
2 tablespoons soft brown sugar
125 g wholemeal flour
75 g butter
2 tablespoons demerara sugar
2 tablespoons muesli

1   Put the banana and pineapple chunks into a large bowl. Add the soft brown sugar and orange rind and mix together well.

2   Grease a pie dish with some butter and spread the fruit mix in the dish.

3 Put the flour and butter in to another dish. Cut the butter into little pieces then rub it into the flour with your fingers until it looks like crumbs.

4 Add the demerara sugar and muesli and mix together well.

5 Spoon the crumble mix over the fruit. Bake in the oven at 190° Centigrade (375° Fahrenheit, gas mark 5) for 25–30 minutes.

Serve hot with yoghurt or cream.

Glossary

acidity The level of acid that a substance contains.
airtight Sealed so that air cannot get in or out.
allergy A bad reaction to some substances, such as foods.
Amerindians American Indians, the original peoples of America.
bacteria Tiny plants that can cause disease but can also be useful.
calories Measurements of the energy in food.
carbohydrate Starchy or sugary foods which give us energy.
cholesterol A substance found in our bodies and in some foods.
classical From ancient Greece or Rome.
coat of arms A picture that represents a certain family.
compost Soil or other material where plants can grow.
cosmetics Products to make people look more attractive.
crystallized Preserved and covered with sugar.
distilled A process of heating then cooling liquids.
environment The landscape and the animals, plants and people who live there.
ferment A chemical change which can be caused or speeded up by adding live yeast or bacteria.
fertility The ability of a plant or animal to produce young.
fertilized When female and male parts have joined together to make seed or young.
fertilizer A substance used on crops to feed the plants.
fibre Part of food which helps us to digest it and pass it through our bodies.
folklore Stories, legends and myths from a certain area or culture.
grove A small wood.
hot houses Heated buildings for growing plants.
kernel The edible centre inside a nut shell or fruit stone.
legend A traditional myth or story.
medieval from the period of the Middle Ages.
meditated When someone has thought deeply about something.
Middle Ages The time in history from the fifth to the fifteenth century.
minerals Substances found in some foods that we need to keep us healthy.
mythology The tradition of stories from a certain culture or area.
Norse From ancient Scandinavia.
nutrients Substances in food which we need to keep us healthy.
nutritious Containing goodness.

organic Produced without the use of chemicals.
Pilgrim Fathers A group of people who sailed from England to America and set up a community at Massachusetts in 1620.
plantations Large estates of land where crops are grown.
pollen Fine grains of powder from the male part of a flower.
preserve To prepare something so that it will keep fresh in storage.
processing Preparing products.
protein Part of food we need to build and repair our bodies.
pruned Cut back.
spirits Strong alcoholic drinks made by distillation.
temperate A region or climate that is never very hot or cold.
Thanksgiving A celebration, first started by the Pilgrim Fathers, that takes place in the USA.
tropical A region or climate that has high temperatures and heavy rainfall.
vats Tanks, usually used for holding liquid.
vineyard A plantation of grape vines, usually for wine making.
vitamins Substances found in some foods which we need to keep us healthy.
wholesalers Traders who buy in large quantities and sell on to supermarkets and shops.

Books to read

Focus on Fruit by Graham Houghton (Wayland, 1986)
Fruit by Jacqueline Dineen (Young Library, 1987)
Fruit by Miriam Moss (A & C Black, 1991)
Let's Visit a Fruit Farm by Sarah Doughty and Diana Bentley (Wayland, 1989)
Nuts by Catherine Chambers (Evans Brothers Ltd., 1995)

You may find some of the older books listed above in your local library.

For further information on fruit, contact:
The Fresh Fruit and Vegetable Information Service,
Bury House,
126–128 Cromwell Road,
London SW7 4ET

Index

Numbers in **bold** show subjects that appear in pictures.

Africa 21, 22
ancient Egyptians **6**
ancient Greeks 6
ancient Romans 6, 24
animals 5, **10**
Arabia 24
Australia **16**

bacteria 16, 17
baking **20**, 20
birds 5, 10
birthdays 9
biscuits 18, 20
bottling fruit 17
Buddha 24
Buddhists 24

cakes 5, 7, 9, 18, 23
candied fruits 17, 23
canning 9, **17**, 17
Caribbean 21, 22
China 24, 25
Christians 24
Christmas 9
chutneys 17
cooking fruit 20–21, 22–23
crystallized fruit 17
curries 21, 23

doctors 7, 8
dried fruits 6, 7, **13**, **16**, 16, **18**, 18, 23
drinks 5, 13, **18**, 18, **19**, 19, 25

England 9, 19

fairy tales 24
festivals 24
fools 18
France 7, **9**, 19
freezing 17

Germany 17, 22
Greece 25
growing fruit 6, 9, 10, **14–15**, 14–15

Hallowe'en 24
harvesting 15
Hindus 24
ice-cream 18, 20
India 21, 25
Italy **14**

jams 7, 17, 18, **19**, 19
Japan **14**
jellies 5, 7, 18, 20, 21
Jews 25

legends 24

marmalade 8, 17, 18
medicine 7
Mexico 22
Middle East 21, 23
minerals 12
Morocco 23
mousses 18, 20
myths 24

New Year 25
nuts 5, 5, 6, 10, 13, 19, 20, 21, 22

pickles 17
pies 5, 7, 18, 20, 22
Pilgrim Fathers 7
plague 7
poaching 20
preserving 6, 9, **16–17**, 16–17
processing 15, 18–19

recipes 26–29

sailors 8
salads 5, 20, 23
sauces 18, 20, 21
Scandinavia 22
scurvy 8
seeds 4, 10, 11
soups 5, 21, 22
South America 9
Spain 25
stewing 20
stews 5, 7, 21, 22
sweets 20

tarts 18
Thanksgiving 7, 24
tropical fruits 9, **10**, 10

USA 7, 19, 24

vegetables 4
vegetarians 13
vineyards 7, **9**
vitamins 8, 12, 13

wassailing **25**, 25
weddings 9
West Indies 9, 17, 21, 23
wine 6, 7, 8, 9, 15